ALL WOMEN ARE BITCHES, AND ALL MEN ARE BASTARDS

NINA VAN DER PLAS

BALBOA.
PRESS

A DIVISION OF HAY HOUSE

Balboa Press books may be ordered through booksellers or by contacting:

Balboa Press
A Division of Hay House
1663 Liberty Drive
Bloomington, IN 47403
www.balboapress.com.au
1-(877) 407-4847

ISBN: 978-1-4525-0673-9 (sc)
ISBN: 978-1-4525-0674-6 (e)

Printed in the United States of America

Balboa Press rev. date: 08/22/2012

CONTENTS

DOES FAIRY TALE TRULY EXIST?

There are so many stories of the knight in shining armour coming to claim or rescue the princess and live happily ever after. The fairy tale *is* true; the writers just forgot to Tell us about the responsibility each person has in the relationship to make it blossom.

In society, men and women are being taught how to harden themselves against feeling, making the world more and more masculine and less and less feminine. Trusting intuition is left to a select few, and as this happens, the relationships between men and women get harder to maintain.

Feminine energy and masculine energy are equally important. As one goes out and gets, the other nurtures and supports. One is of the mind, the other of the body.

Did you ever notice that when a woman approaches a man in her masculine energy, she immediately calls him to combat? A classic example of this would be a woman approaching a man from an aggressive position, the reaction or response is most likely going to be matched with his own aggression, irritation or agitation.

But when she approaches the man in her more feminine energy (through feeling), she invites him to open his heart, and the man is then called to act, support, and protect. This type of approach comes from a place that empowers both people in this situation. Both men and women carry masculine and feminine energy, this is important, as balance can be achieved when we honour them both.

Everything works in balance. What we have learned through our childhood is naturally played out in our adult lives. The more aware of ourselves we become, the easier it is to break these patterns. If your mum or dad was "weak" in your eyes, you may be determined, whether it be consciously or unconsciously motivated, to be the exact opposite. By focusing on what you don't want, you create that very thing because you fail to acknowledge what you do in fact want! It becomes a vicious circle.

Something such as a simple change in focus can be the start to a new way of being. This can be difficult, as relationships are challenged and either grow stronger or move in the opposite direction. The old saying, "it's better than nothing," tends to come into play here. Or, "At least I have someone to be with, and I am not alone!"

If we loved ourselves enough, we would never allow ourselves to be miserable, hurt, or sad. So I ask you this: would you fight for love, or would you fight for fear? Fight for love, and your life changes in profound ways, with the endless possibilities of deep love. Fight for fear, and you stay where you are, with the possibilities of becoming unhappier and more fearful.

Another question to ask yourself is: "What do I really want for myself?" Consider no one else; what would you as a unique individual want for yourself? By doing this, you effectively honour not only yourself by speaking your truth, but you honour everyone around you by not naively speaking on their behalf.

Many people will put everyone else's needs before their own. Unfortunately, this tendency lends itself to a habitual behaviour that means you never get or do what you truly desire. And even worse, you could end up feeling like you are the victim of all these situations!

The truth is that the choices you've made have resulted in everything you have in this moment—from the life you lead and the money you have, to the partner you are with. The concept of the "victim" is flawed, more often than not we are only victims of ourselves . . . no one else.

Knowing this very empowering piece of information, it is easier to understand the concept of "we get what we believe we deserve." If you believe that you deserve second best (even if you claim otherwise), then that is what you will get. Saying and believing are very different, we may know that we deserve the best, but if you subliminally do not believe that to be the case, you will only ever allow yourself second best.

The people we attract: friends, lovers, partners, are all reflections of who we are, in that there are qualities in them that we recognise in ourselves. This is where compassion comes from, an understanding of what someone shows you of themselves, and you recognise it through your own experiences of that feeling, belief, situation etc.

For example: You say you believe you deserve the best partner in the world, yet you do not believe it. You will seek the best and end up with less than, this partner will mirror to you or reflect back to you exactly what you believe you deserve and they will treat you accordingly.

So the importance of knowing what you deeply desire as a unique individual is truly profound! Once you have sat down and worked out what it is that *you* want, sit with your partner and discuss with him or her what it is that you want for yourself. Invite your partner to do the same.

We come into a relationship as independent individuals, so why do we forfeit this individuality for fear of losing the other person when what attracted that person to us in the first place were our unique qualities? Maintaining your individuality is absolutely key to maintaining a solid relationship that is unless you want to be co-dependent.

Now let's look at the age-old problem:
The man believes the woman is trying to change him.
Where does this come from?

This behaviour, we are all aware, stems from the same place that settling for second best does . . . a lack of self-love. When a woman is not being loved in the way she wants or desires, she will naturally encourage the man to step up—which means change! This happens on an unconscious level, so she won't even realize she is doing it. She will only realize that she is unhappy in her relationship and will place the blame on him.

This would not happen if she loved herself completely, as she would then choose to be with a man who reflected what she yearned for. In this space, she is again honouring herself, because she (like the man she is with) will only accept the best. It is never easy, because life is a wonderful journey full of learning and change, but the bliss is well worth it!

Whereas the woman does choose a man who matches her in that love space, the man chooses a woman he doesn't believe he truly deserves. Reflections of self-worth in both partners are now very apparent. His struggle to feel love often comes out in a passive-aggressive victim-type approach, and the woman's demeanour becomes aggressive, never satisfied with what she gets. Both partners are then unhappy, because both behaviours come from unworthiness.

So many people get caught up in the potential of others that they forget to see what the reality of the situation really is. Women are terrible culprits of this; I was one of them, until recently!

An example of this is an experience I had with an ex-partner of mine. He was a beautiful man, who was terrified of feeling. I wanted a deeper connection, which meant the need to feel and let go of fear; as one person changes, so too does everyone else around that person. In saying that, the choices we make offer the opportunity for everyone around to make their own choices which is where the "everyone else" changes around me/you becomes a true statement. Relationships and people change from the important decisions we make. The more I opened up to what I wanted, the more he shut down or closed himself off to me. It was very painful but enriching in so many ways.

I received an ultimatum from him three months out from our wedding: I had to choose between being with him or having a family. I couldn't believe it: the dream was destroyed. I was still caught up in the *potential* of him, as opposed to the *reality* of him. He had two children from a previous relationship and prior to us making wedding arrangements, we had both agreed to try for one child together. Unfortunately, this agreement changed, and it was better to find out before, rather than after the wedding.

I saw his potential as an amazing father, and the possibility to have a stress-free mind and life. The reality was that he would fight for fear and not love; the reality was, that he chose to stay asleep. I have since promised to see things as they are, not for what they could be. This means I don't miss out on what happens now, because I am always in the present moment. The past and future are concepts of the mind, after all.

So to help break this pattern, try working out what it is that *you* truly want. It is a great place to start, and wonderful things happen to those who have the courage to follow it through.

Now to address the next age-old problem:
Possessive men who try to change or control the women they love. Why does this happen?

If I am completely honest, my relationship history has been marked by possessive men. I must admit, it took me a while to work it out, but, my Lord, am I pleased I woke up to it!

I am not a jealous woman by any means; I love seeing people enjoying themselves, and I am fiercely loyal and faithful. However, I do believe in freedom. Men of my past are all attracted to me because of my sense of light, love, and freedom, (very hippie, I know). But it was these qualities that attracted them that they were petrified of in themselves.

An example of this was a conversation I had with one of my exes one day. "Anything is possible," I said.

"No, it's not. How can it be? Unless you can afford to, have the certificate or know someone . . . it is purely luck that that will determine whether "anything" is possible." he said.

Despite the love and genuine knowledge of how loyal and faithful I am to them, they just couldn't cope with my sense of freedom and absolutely anything being possible. So what happened?

The controlling man has an "ideal" that a woman should be like, so he will attempt to "mould" her, so as to control her and effectively keep her. The key words here are "keep her." This type of man is so damn scared that he may lose this woman that instead of embracing this feeling of love, bliss, and freedom, he chooses to restrain her (which she allows; remember, it takes two to tango), hoping she never leaves. If she leaves, and in my case, each time I did, the man lets her go in the end. He does not fight for her, as a man would. Common reasons why a man lets a woman go like this are; he has to start taking responsibility for his actions and manipulations, he would have to start to accept her for who she really is, and finally she won't bow down to his games of control anymore, which ultimately means that the relationship would no longer be run by fear. By the woman walking away she sends the message that she won't accept being treated in that manner anymore. Men embodying true masculine energy are not afraid of love; they fight for it. And they fight for life.

Now let's look at a different approach to relationship, but one that boils down to the same thing each time: The man and woman choose partners that reflect how much they don't think they deserve. Unworthiness!

Please be very clear on this: When in a relationship, each one of the partners involved is responsible for his or her situation. If a woman comes in and tries to change the man and the man complies, albeit unhappily, he has still chosen to comply with her demands, and consequently, they are both perpetrators.

If the man wishes to keep the woman by controlling her and she complies, they are both perpetrators; he pushed and she said yes. It takes two to tango, everything that happens, happens because you AGREED to it! If you didn't agree to it, you would have stopped it or left it.

To Summarize: People are amazing creatures, constantly evolving and reaching new heights. What we need to do to get what we want is pay attention to the now in the present, know what we really want, live in love (not fear), and stand strong in our own truth.

Granted this is easier said than done, but if you make a consistent effort, you won't believe the kind of bliss and happiness that will flow to you in abundant loads!

Am I A Control Freak?
Surely not!

Ever wondered why people are so obsessed with keeping everything in their little world in "perfect" order? What are they scared of? What are they trying to prevent? Why do they worry about the past and how it will affect their future? What is it that they are trying so hard to control that they end up never controlling it at all?

If you answered yes to any of these questions you may find yourself struggling when things seem out of your control. Yes we have all had experiences where we end up in "fretville" but that is a part of being human. It is not wrong or bad, it simply *just is* and the key is to be aware of it when it happens. Awareness means you can start to change patterns that no longer serve you instead of allowing them to persist.

Now if you have to be in control, this does not make you the manipulative archenemy of mankind, it simply means that at this present time in your life, you are run by fear. Fear of the "what if"!

Truth is, I used to be a huge worrywart. If it wasn't what people thought of me that I was worried about, it was what I needed to do to make sure what was going to happen next actually happened and that was the only way that I felt safe!

Being a worrywart, and many people are self-confessed culprits, means that through fear, we try to control that which is completely out of our control—life and other people. Safeties, fear, past, and future are all concepts of the mind. They keep us preoccupied over things we cannot control, which keep us completely out of the present moment. Think about it; if we are truly safe and secure, what if a natural disaster like a hurricane came through unexpectedly and took your home? What if you turned up to work to find the company had gone bankrupt? Nothing is secure and safe; we simply have to work with what we are given and be present enough to see what is coming (without letting fear control us). And only then will we be able to handle the things that come at us that are completely out of our control.

The other problem with this condition is that by being concerned or paranoid about a negative outcome, we naturally attract it to us, because that is all we have focused on! Change the mindset and you change the way you approach life. Through a positive mind change, we start to focus on what we do want, thus manifesting what we would like to see rather than what we don't. We are all very powerful manifestors; everything we have right now is because of the choices we have made, which directly reflect our belief in ourselves and life. If you want to see positive change, it isn't just a case of how much you think and say something. Words are just empty. The change won't happen until you truly know and believe it.

For example, if a man goes into an interview saying he is worth one million dollars, but deep down he only thinks he is worth fifty thousand, guess what salary that individual is going to get. Fifty thousand, of course! If he truly believed he was worth more, he would NOT accept less and would have found a job worth one million.

The laws of attraction do work and work very well. The key, as mentioned in the above paragraph, is that you know and believe in what you are thinking into reality. If you only think it but don't believe/know it . . . well, it just won't happen because you are really expecting the opposite (believing the negative to happen).

A person who suffers with issues around control will naturally believe the worst is going to happen (most of the time) and therefore "think" it into fruition! And voilà! There is your negative experience just as you predicted!

Either way you are a success, because what you willed to happen did. Well done!

Ask anyone who worries or struggles to be in control and they will tell you about the pressures of doing the right thing and being a good person they place on themselves and the consequences of this! This kind of pressure results in high stress and high stress wreaks havoc on the body; the following are just some of the conditions that have been attributed to stress:

- Hives
- Burn out
- Nervous breakdown

- Pimples
- Psoriasis
- Cold sores
- Hair loss
- Sleep deprivation
- Weight loss
- Weight gain

Control and Relationships

Now that you can start to understand the stress and unhappiness that worry and control wreak on the individual, you can start to see and feel how this would affect the person in relationships. Relationships include love, work, and friendship.

For someone to be ruled by fear, that person's ability to be open when it comes to feeling, exploring, and risk is incredibly limited! Most of these individuals struggle to just be on their own because they don't have enough distraction to keep their mind occupied with things that stop them from worrying, etc. Time with yourself, the most important person in your life,—who could have thought it could be so difficult? Or even boring?

This becomes quite crippling in a love relationship as everything needs to be a certain way in relation to an ideal the person has pictured in his or her mind as to how the perfect life should look. This in no way denotes the controlling or worrisome individual as the bad guy or gal causing problems in the relationship. Again, it is a two-way street; if things you do not like are happening . . .

it is because you agreed to let it happen! If you didn't want it to continue, you would have stopped it or left the situation.

So how do we turn a worrywart into a carefree individual?
How do we assist the one who "has" to be in control to let go of the reigns?

These changes are not easy and do take time and commitment, and I can tell you it is well and truly worth it! Here are some ideas on what you can do to influence positive change in your life.

First, you need to start paying attention to how you react out of habit to certain stimulus (this is different for everyone).

Secondly, once you have started to see what it is that triggers you, look at ways you can start to breathe and feel through the situation before you react. This will start you in beginning changes; the more you pay attention, the easier it becomes and the greater the changes you notice.

For those who have very active minds, going to guided meditations, yoga, or just finding a quiet place to reflect on a regular basis all can do wonders.

Remember, there is nothing wrong with anyone who suffers from these traits. Simply becoming more aware of them makes life just that little bit easier.

Control comes in many forms, as you are starting to see. It can be that you like things your way all the time. It could be that you are used to having a lot of structure and logic in your life. Or you are used to forcing the ideal of safety and security, hoping that by making it happen, it will in fact stay that way.

A great illusion, this concept of the mind only serves to blind us from what is really happening around us in the moment. Again, fretting about the past and future means that you miss out on the now. The past and future are concepts of the mind, after all. One has been and gone . . . cannot be changed. The other is yet to happen and cannot be seen as yet.

So our choices lie in our awareness of ourselves and our want to experience everything in the NOW. Do you know what you want? Do you want to live life now? Or do you want to wait until the "right time" comes around? The secret is that the right time is always now.

Is It Really My Fault?

Isn't it funny when things don't go exactly how we would like them to that we start to beat ourselves up for it? Oh I could have done this better, that better . . . maybe if I hadn't said that, things would be different? Honestly, if it was meant to workout, it would have. The age-old cliché "everything happens for a reason" is so true that it is annoying!

I had an experience recently that had a profound effect on the way I see myself and myself in relationships. It woke me up and made me very clear on what I wanted for myself in a relationship, and that was just awesome. The process it took to get there was very painful, but oh so worth it.

When it came to decision time, I had to be clear on what I deeply wanted and it came to light very quickly that what I wanted was very different to what he wanted. He was scared of a deeper connection because of the self-responsibility it comes with, whereas I was not afraid and wanted to delve into the depth of connection one could have with another. It took four months to get here to this realization.

The painful part of this experience came from the lack of communication and there was an avoidance of this from both parties. I didn't know what the hell the relationship was and he didn't either, but at first, we were willing to explore and have some great fun!

By the time I had made my decision (about three weeks before we actually talked about what we do from that point on), our relationship had already started to change. Amazing how connected we all are; as the saying goes: "as one changes, so does everyone else around them." We all have an effect on people and it is with this knowledge and understanding that we are able to then understand why, when someone pulls away in a relationship, the other reaches out to them to pull them back in. By reacting out of fear, we avoid having to feel loss, pain or abandonment.

When I felt the change in him, I didn't know what to think or feel. The lack of communication was the killer and I wasn't very vocal on my side of the court, which didn't help either. I was confused, despite knowing what I had to do. I felt maybe I had offended him, maybe he didn't find me attractive anymore, and heaven forbid . . . maybe he was not satisfied in our intimate moments.

This was a new experience for me, I really liked him and never had I questioned myself like this, with undermining, self-criticizing, and negative thoughts. Those issues I had created in my own mind had never been questioned in the past, so why now?

There was just nothing but assumption. We had to talk about it, and during our chat we discovered in that moment just how much we wanted different things in life. We had to acknowledge these differences, respect them and start to make plans to move on.

It was painful for both of us, he wanted to be a "single" couple with his children from a previous marriage and I wanted to have both his children and my own. I wanted a partner who wanted to share that unique and special experience with me.

Self expression is not only incredibly important in all relationships, it is very healing. Through our chat in the example I have given you, we both gained huge clarity around his lack of honesty around what he really wanted, but also how much I needed to meet someone who shared the same sense of life and adventure that I do. I followed my intuition and my heart. It was truly a gift. Now, when in the midst of what can become a very heated conversation, remember, that when you talk, it is about you, not the other person. For example, say things like "I feel that . . ."

Never run in as the accuser wanting to blame with "you did this, you made me feel." The fact is NO ONE CAN MAKE YOU FEEL ANYTHING! This approach will only end up in tears; we are adults after all, aren't we?! So let's approach the situation like adults as opposed to schoolyard children.

My take on this whole experience has been that we are each our own best and worst friend, hero and villain. In a relationship, it takes two to create what is and two to change it. It is neither one nor the other's fault as whatever they did, each agreed because that person stayed to see it happen, and visa versa.

We all create what we believe we deserve. Look at your life as it is now; look at the things, people, all the aspects you do and don't like about your life, and then think about this statement: Everything you have right here right now is a result of your own choices!!!

You can create a life you want, you can have anything you want. You just have to go out and get it! If we get out of our own way every once in a while, we may actually realize both what we want and how to get there. Life is only as hard as you make it.

Just like the people who say they always get the broken item in the shop, the people I speak of create success through the failure they set themselves up for. By focusing on the negative, they create it, which makes it a success, because they got exactly what they "knew" would happen.

Beating yourself up for things past only holds you back there in that moment; it does not serve you and help you move forward. In fact, if we are left to dwell, it will result in the same experience over and over until we learn our lesson and get out of that cycle! Not easy but well worth it.

Stand up for yourself, speak, and honour truth. It's up to you!

Why is Getting What You Want So Bloody Difficult?

We all have goals, wants, needs, and dreams. So why don't we just go and get them? Do you notice how some people seem to have it all while others constantly seem to suffer? How is this right? Where is the balance?

Well here is the truth of the matter: everything you have right now you created! Yes that is right; everything you have right now is a result of your choices. So if you are not happy with what you have currently created for yourself . . . change it!

This is easier said than done, as this means a whole change in how we see ourselves and how we approach life. If we are consistent, however, it can and will happen. We all have the ability and deserve to have everything we want; we just have to believe it and then put it into action!

So how do you begin to change your current way of being to get this? Firstly, we need to have a look at why you don't believe you deserve this level of happiness. Let's be honest, if you truly believed you deserved a greater level of happiness, you would have it already! This is where actions speak louder than words; what you say should always be backed up by what you do. If you say "I love myself" and then go out and get blind drunk, sleep with someone, and feel like crap the following morning for what you did, then you just showed how much you don't love yourself.

If you truly loved yourself, you would never hurt yourself or do anything that would result in you becoming sad or unhappy. You can now start to see why this process can be very confronting. When you are taking yourself through this process, you will come up against a few things about you that you won't want to acknowledge—we all have those things. The most common of these is the "victim" complex.

We all know at least one person who embodies this; it may even be us! The only reason we know of this type of behaviour is because we have either been it, are it, or have seen it. Always remember: everything we like or dislike in another is a reflection of what we like or dislike in ourselves! It is a hard truth, but we can only experience life from our own perspective allowing us to only know and experience things that reside within ourselves.

The victim is a passive-aggressive manipulator who gains attention and favours through his or her sad stories or unfortunate set of circumstances. This draws those who want to save others into helping that person. The victim truly believes that he or she is a "victim of circumstance."

There is no such thing as a victim of circumstance; everything you have right now is a result of your own choices.

These 'victims' are not bad or evil; most of them are unaware that they even do this. On a deeper level they really do not believe they deserve the love and attention they look for, so they play the 'helpless victim' which is a passive aggressive way of getting more attention to prove to themselves time and time again that people do actually love them. They are often the people who play on the "feel sorry for me" card and as a result others drop what they are doing to help them.

This behaviour is insatiable and the victim always needs feedback in order to feel good about his or herself. The concept of "you don't know what you don't know" is very true of all of life's lessons. Like most "victims," who are unaware of what they are doing, those who struggle with issues around control, abandonment, and loss could very well be in the same boat. Understanding this means that we can have compassion for them with the hope that they will wake up to themselves. Everyone deserves to be loved!

Everyone in every moment of life is presented with a choice: a choice to go to work, a choice to invest in developing him or herself, and a choice to have compassion and be self-responsible. Everyone can choose to change if they want to and believe they can do it.

With choice comes responsibility. If people choose not to move forward and work on themselves, change their patterns of behaviour, it is their choice. They are obviously happy to remain as they are so you should accept them as they are. Being honest as a friend, lover, or colleague is all you can be (with love). It doesn't make the individual any better or worse as a person, the individual just don't want what you want for her or himself. Anyone who loves helping people, not saving them from themselves, will be all too aware of this. The person wishing to save people from themselves has a value system caught up in the success of the "victim," choosing to actualize that person's potential. When the "victim" chooses not to, the whole world around the "saviour" comes crashing down!

No one should wear the burdens of anyone else; self-responsibility means that each is responsible for his or her problems or situation. You have a whole life's work ahead of you saving yourself from yourself, how the hell do you have time to save anyone else?

Trying to save someone neither helps nor honours anyone involved. The "victim" does not have to address his or her problems and becomes more ignorant, and the saviour gets bogged down with the weight of the world because that is what that person signed up for. You can still be friends; you just need to be clear on what you are happy to take on or not. True respect is formed when people are honest (with love) and own what it is they truly are and want.

Those who choose to address their behaviour will go through a transformative journey challenging everything they know to be the truth in their world. They are suddenly being introduced to self-responsibility. Self-responsibility is the acceptance of all that you have created, done, and experienced. For example, notice how you react to someone when that person points out something that challenges you. No one can make you feel anything; how you choose to react is your choice and your responsibility—no one else's.

We have all had challenging experiences and our friends can be amazing teachers for us. We all know someone who would fall into the "victim" category and other friends who would fall into the "saviour" category of wanting to save the victim from pain. It is the ultimate cat and mouse game; it is very easy to get caught up in it and each party is as bad as the other.

Firstly, you need to understand the role the saviour plays in this situation. The saviour wants to help people, but instead of insisting people wear their own burdens and become more self-responsible, the saviour unconsciously go into the role of trying to save the victim from feeling his or her own pain as a way of hopefully making it all better. This never works as the weight of the world is the worn on the saviour's shoulders until such time as that person get sicks of it and reacts. Things then don't usually end well.

The problem with this is that it does not honour everyone in the situation. The victim does not learn or grow from the experience and neither does the saviour. Everyone needs to be able to make a conscious choice to be more self-responsible.

Secondly, you need to look at the play between victim and saviour as a triangle. At each of the points there is victim, saviour, and perpetrator. When the interactions between the victim and the saviour get to be too much, the saviour reacts saying, "enough is enough," and the victim reacts to the saviour as if they are the bad parent: "you don't love me." Thus the saviour becomes the perpetrator. At this point, normally the saviour feels guilty for how he or she treated the victim, which is worsened by the cold shoulder the saviour often gets through this time. Then the saviour works to make things 'all better' so that victim and saviour become friends again and the cycle starts over.

In order to change the way in which a relationship works, you first need to look at yourself and realize what it is that you are doing that is causing this to happen for you . . . not them, you. When you work out where this behaviour stems from, you can start to request a change in the way people interact with you. You will notice as you become more aware of yourself just how much people change around you anyway.

When you find yourself in a situation like this, learning how to cope when the other person or people involved make their choices on how to react is vital. What the individual chooses to do with that information is that person's choice. So when you invite someone to interact with you differently, that individual will either embrace the adult within and step up or that individual will embrace the child within and stay at the same place. Neither one is right or wrong

Their choice is their choice and it is up to everyone to have compassion and understanding. If they choose to react, it often comes in the form of accusation. And if you can see the big picture, you see that it is a way for the individual to deal with the hurt that person feels by effectively blaming someone else for it.

We cannot control how people react, we can only speak our truth (with love), honouring everyone involved. Living to please other people only serves to dishonour your own individual wants and needs and thus dishonour those around you as you refrain from speaking your truth.

When you are honest and express this honesty with love, you will always get what you want deep down in the end!

SOME PEOPLE JUST CAN'T!

Have you ever met someone who has all the opportunity and endless possibilities at his or her fingertips? Most people would answer, "All the time."

Regardless of whether you are having sessions with someone to get you heading in the right path, seeking advice from a friend, or just simply weighing up your options, you have the choice to move forward and the choice to stay where you are.

While training people in fitness, I found it was much the same. When you are working with your client figuring out their goals and underlying reason for coming to see you, you come to a fork in the road. This is where the client chooses to go forward and commit to change, or go forward and hope that change occurs without his or her input.

Obviously, one choice is more preferred to the other. However, when it comes down to it, whichever path becomes the chosen one to go down will determine a completely different outcome for the individual. So that person needs to be very clear on what it is he or she is about to decide on. As they say, "an educated decision is always better than one that isn't educated."

The feeling or concept of "just can't" is very real in some people. They just don't have the necessary tools at this time to be able to alter the way everything is for them, despite knowing it could be different. They might even spend time, as mentioned earlier, with various therapists, friends, work, and even study, but they never seem to be any the wiser.

A sense of hopelessness can present itself, but ultimately acceptance is the key here to a happier way of being. Having people like us around who are optimistic, full of hope, explorers of possibilities and opportunities, is fantastic as the world needs people like us. We need to have compassion, though, for those who despite the want to make things happen for themselves, just don't have the necessary tools available to them that can make it happen.

The approach they need to take, through the support of their friends, work, study, therapist, etc., is to just keep on working toward what they want and place no pressure on themselves in regards to the end result. Small goals and steps should be put in place with realistic goals being the main objective. Anything out of reach or unrealistic only encourages a greater sense of despair.

THE CHOICES WE MAKE

Self-responsibility. Those are a couple of words that today's society has conveniently forgotten or just decided it just doesn't like what they mean.

It seems like today if you want to avoid responsibility, you just blame it on someone else. "That restaurant made my child fat!" "They made me do it."

No one made you do anything; you chose to go in a certain direction and you are responsible for it and the consequences of those actions. Tough I know, but unless you own what it is that you are creating, challenges and all, you will not be able to move forward and into the life you may be dreaming of.

Everything comes to those who take responsibility for their actions and that comes with baring the consequences and working through the tough times as well as the good. It would be great if we only had it easy all the time, but then there would not be any gratitude for what we have. Hence, there is the need for the contrast of challenges so we truly appreciate the great times, relationships, promotions, and abundance.

"All Women are Bitches and All Men Are Bastards!"

Feminism: The word that strikes fear into the hearts of all men.

Now the original point behind the whole feminist movement was to increase the rights of women, which is the best thing that ever happened for us. Unfortunately, today it has got a little out of hand, so much so that a man can't even open the door for a woman without being told, "I can do it myself."

This doesn't always happen, but it is common. A man nowadays cannot offer the courtesies of old without a woman thinking he is suggesting she cannot do it herself. This may seem harsh in its tone, but it is the reality of the way things are. Yes, as women we are very fortunate to have the freedoms we do. However, we must wake up to the fact that when men offer their support or service, whether it be carrying something for us or opening the car door, they are offering because they want to help and enjoy looking after us.

Men are not all assholes just as women are not all bitches. We attract what we expect and what we think we deserve.

Women are beautiful creatures; we are in touch with our emotions, we feel deeply, and some of us even trust our innate intuition. To men this is completely illogical and lacks structure, hence stress sometimes arises when women and men try to communicate. We, men and women, are trying to say the same thing, just in a different language. Man is of the mind and woman is of the body.

Women of today have not been brought up to be partners to their men; they have not been brought up to be able cope with hurt and to work with it in an adult way. Most adults are really children trapped in adult bodies. Harsh reality? Of course it is. Anyone who is adult by age would like to think of him or herself as mature, but if you look at the way we react to hurt from the opposite sex, friends, and work colleagues, you would soon discover the possible lack of maturity in yourself or someone else.

This is very important when it comes to interrelating. For example, he cheats on you and you react by divorcing or breaking up with him whilst trying to take everything he has because you have been together for over four years. Hate is purely a reaction to how much we truly love someone; the more we love them the more we react out of spite and hatred when we lack the maturity to handle the situation as an adult should.

I am not saying you should walk away from everything; make sure you walk away cared for. Just have compassion for yourself in that situation and also for the other person. It is far better and easier maintaining a relationship that is in good terms than that of bitterness and hatred. It only breeds negativity and encourages the same thing to repeat in your next relationship and so on and so forth. This is where the cliché "all men are bastards" comes from. Women end up in these situations that are reactive again and again, causing couples to fail in their ability to deal with the situation as adults. Consequently, it becomes another unhappy ending with another partner, forever in your black list of people never to get along with again.

Now, every relationship involves two people and both of them contribute equally to the outcome of all situations they find themselves in. It is never ONE person's fault!

Men today are not taught or brought up in society being encouraged to be in touch with their feelings and emotions. They are taught that to feel loved and to be a man you have to have sex, and the more sex you have the more of a man you are. The problem here is that instead of being taught to not fear feelings and to surrender to the beauty of the woman when making love, they are taught that it is a conquest and void-filling exercise, which is insatiable. To find love, you have to first discover love within yourself! This void-filling exercise is true of both men and women. There is a cliché from woman to woman that goes, "all my sex for just one hug." So as much as men have been blamed for using women for sex in the past, it is equally true of women today as well. Women more than ever use sex to feel loved in a similar fashion to which men have used sex to feel loved. This is a void filling exercise that is insatiable and until they address the issues of self-love, neither men nor women will ever experience the love they crave on the level they deeply desire.

Through sex, a woman's heart opens and through the woman, a man's heart opens, and they both experience love. So it is not too hard to see why sex is addictive. When it is the only way someone can feel that euphoria, until they can find it in themselves, they will engage sexually with as many people as they can to get that satisfaction.

Men and women, when they are not open to feelings and feeling, have a limited experience of love through sex. Making love or sex is the ultimate surrender of one person to another, a true heart opening experience. For people to experience love in the way they truly yearn for, they must first discover that love for themselves. If you truly loved yourself you would never hurt yourself or put yourself through anything that would make you upset or unhappy. No one would "settle"!

So sadly the whole concept of "men are bastards" comes from the lack of men's want or ability to get in touch with their feelings (often as a result of fear). And because of this, these men are driven to seek love through whatever means will satisfy them. The relationships they seek and endure become that purely of the flesh, this is the same for both men and women. Feelings are important and to have intimacy in a relationship we must be able to talk or express ourselves freely; which means getting in touch with our feelings. Intimacy is one of the hardest things to achieve as it asks for raw honesty and vulnerability, and for the cases mentioned above, both the man and the woman will continue to search for that sense of wholeness through the flesh because it seems like a more fun and easy option, never to be satisfied.

Both men and women simply want to experience love and if they can keep on experiencing it through themselves and then through partnership, the contentment they seek will be truly abundant. The key here is to look to yourself before looking for someone else to make you feel good or complete. You are complete as an individual and do not need anyone to feel love, and by experiencing this of yourself, you open yourself up to the kind of relationship with the love you yearn for.

This can be a scary experience but the bliss is truly worth it!

THE TRUE MEANING
OF LOVE

Love: the dream, the fantasy, the yearning.

Deep down we all know what it is and where it comes from, yet as soon as we are offered the opportunity to experience and embrace it, we get scared! Suddenly, the bliss of new love is overshadowed by this fear of being vulnerable; for fear of losing that special somebody.

Being vulnerable means letting go of the fear of loss, grief, and sadness to experience greater bliss. However, most of us decide to choose the other option. This "other" option is based in fear and results in reactive tendencies placing rules and ownership over things and people as a way of keeping things the way they are.

Let's be real for a moment. No one owns or possesses anyone. We do not have that right and marriage does not mean your life ends because of a contract; it is simply a celebration of the love two people have for one another. Somehow, it has become a way of people stamping their ownership over another in order to further "secure" what that person sees as "their" future together.

This is both suffocating and debilitating for the individuals involved., Because instead of keeping the flame of love alight through freedom, loyalty, living life, and love, the lovers choose to buy into their own expectations of the other partner, rather than what the other partner actually offers.

Love has no strings attached; it is unconditional and if both partners come into a relationship full of love for themselves, they will attract a partner who reflects this. The successful lovers do not need each other; they simply want and yearn for each other. Partners need to communicate what they want in order to be completely happy in their relationship. Without knowing or expressing this, the relationship will eventually and naturally consume the individuals, and their identities will become more and more enmeshed.

SAFETY AND SECURITY: THE LIE THAT IS!

There is a common belief in this day and age that if we have a job, a car, a house, and a family, then all is perfect and the better our ranking in "society." We have been conditioned by the media and other passed-on messages and stories that this is the way it should be if you want to be seen as successful and secure in what you have.

The problem with this is that there is no flexibility and it takes away from the beauty that is life. If we look at it from the point of view that nothing is really secure, safe, and within our control except our reactions, this will make sense.

If you have a job, fantastic; you work hard, you get paid, and all is seemingly well. Then suddenly redundancy (where the company you work for cuts a position they believe they can't afford to keep) occurs and you are left without a position that earns you money. Then Mother Nature pipes up and sends a tornado and your house is destroyed; now you are homeless. So, as you can see, while this is a drastic example, anything can happen and it is all beyond our control. This is not to be mistaken for a, "what you believe you create" scenario as life is far more complex than that. We only have control over what we think and how we react. Things that happen in life which are beyond our control are often sent to us to teach us something. What we take from those experiences is completely up to us. Having a positive attitude in an experience like this will open doors, whilst a negative one will mean we miss those opportunities for not seeing them.

Have you ever had the same experience over and over? This could be in work, relationships, or life in general. Anything that you are yet to learn from continues to repeat and repeat until you finally see what is happening and choose to change and move forward from that pattern. If you have a job that you are fiercely holding on to and wonder why the last two positions you have been made redundant from? Then look at what you are actively or inactively doing out of fear which is causing the outcomes you don't want to happen actually happen.

The learning here is that all is forever changing and if we desperately hold on to anything, it is almost certain to change. The more we let go of the idea of control, the less resistance we have to the constant change that is going on around us. Control is just a concept of the mind when we are ruled by fear.

Safety and control: these are both concepts of the mind and are both driven by the fear of chaos. Anything out of control means that we cannot see what is coming, which means we cannot perceive any kind of outcome. If we know what is around the corner, we can prepare ourselves. Now this is all good if you trust yourself and your intuition, but we are so conditioned nowadays to logically, intelligently and physically work it out all the time, that our intuition gets pushed by the wayside. We all complain that our gut instinct said to do one thing and we did the opposite, only to get the biggest kick in the pants for not trusting ourselves. We should trust ourselves more and listen to that gut feeling we get. You will be pleasantly surprised at what happens when you do! Feeling and trusting your intuition will always allow you to know what the right options and choices are for you in any given moment.

Have you ever wondered why governments and religions strike fear into the hearts of all their followers? They tell you that if you do this . . . that is surely to happen! And "that" is always bad. People who are ruled by fear are easy to control! Simple. These people say something terrible is about to happen, only to follow it up with a solution as to how they can avoid it. Of course, the people will do what they can to be safer and with the speed that information and news from around the world reaches us nowadays, it literally takes seconds for thousands upon thousands of people to get this information and act!

Again, everyone has a choice as to how he or she responds and reacts to everything he or she encounters. Every individual is also responsible for the choices he or she makes regardless of the consequences and/or outcome. So if someone says "jump" and you ask, "how high," it is your own fault that the outcome is not exactly what you hoped for.

NO ONE CAN MAKE ANYONE ELSE DO ANYTHING! You choose to go with or against the options presented to you.

The way you can fare better in the circle of life is to trust your intuition, have a positive attitude and be smart about the choices you make! Intelligence should always support your gut instincts.

THE PURSUIT OF HAPPINESS

Have you ever noticed how some people seem to always look beyond themselves or seek externally to fill the emptiness, void, or unhappiness they feel? Nothing ever seems to work; they always end up in the same place of dissatisfaction and unhappiness.

As the saying goes, "We don't know what we don't know." This is a true statement and a mildly frustrating one, nonetheless.

Those who seek externally to assist themselves in feeling better about themselves and the life they have created, don't know that by avoiding themselves, they completely miss the point.

They are unhappy, because they avoid looking at themselves for the solution to the problems, issues, or unhappiness they are causing in their own lives.

It is a harsh reality to be confronted with, but ultimately, we are each responsible for our own happiness. The reality is even harder to take when we are honest in whether we actually know what we want. Most of us don't. Most of us haven't even asked this question seriously enough to stop for a couple of minutes and feel through what it is that would actually make us happy. If we each did this, suddenly our awareness, direction, satisfaction, and purpose are all realised. And when you do this, no longer can you play the victim of life and circumstance; you have chosen to be self-responsible and own what it is that you really want. You will be honouring yourself and everyone else around you; maturing into an adult from the adolescent behaviours and attitudes you had held dear until this moment.

This is the fork in the road where an individual will choose to move forward to do the work on him or herself to develop and become a self-responsible adult full of love, or continue in fear and unhappiness, looking outward to fix the problems he or she, him or herself, are responsible for.

The choices are to continue to live life as an irresponsible teenager and complain about how things aren't the way you would like them to be, or to make the choice to become a true adult and discover the true meaning of happiness and love. This is where the phase, "boys in men's bodies and girls in women's bodies" comes from.

Neither choice is right nor wrong; it is simply a case of what an individual is ready and able to do in this life. For those who choose to move forward, having compassion and patience with those who choose to stay is a gift. Those who choose to stay as they are can still discover some sense of self-awareness, and need to learn to remain open to those who choose to move forward, as their change and heightened awareness will often give rise to fears of the people who stay. Essentially, this is how most friendships come to end, or as some people refer to it "we just grew apart."

RESISTANCE IS FUTILE

"Not again!" This is an exclamation we are all too familiar with. Life works in cycles and the less we learn about ourselves in this life, the more we repeat the same story. We end up with the same type of man or woman in a relationship, reliving that same experience. It could also be the same work scenario, or even family. This list goes on!

These sorts of things happen when we ignore our gut instincts (intuition) too. It always seems to be that we get the biggest metaphysical slap when we go against our natural instincts. What is that telling you? Another example of this is when we decide we want something to happen and instead of working hard and letting it unfold as it is meant to, we try to force it. The more you try to "make" it happen, the more it seems to run away from you. This is another example of resistance and ignoring your natural understanding of the situation.

If we weren't so caught up in fear, we would see and hear all the messages we need in order to get exactly what we want. This often takes time and patience but it is truly worth it!

In this day and age, we seem to have lost the ability to trust. Trust in ourselves and that all will work out as it should, so long as we remain aware and self-responsible.

The term resistance refers to anything we force to happen or avoid confronting out of fear of losing control of something. We have all done this, and it is something from time to time regardless of our level of awareness that we will all still do. Resistance stops flow. Have you ever just decided you are going to say YES to opportunity and go with it? What happened? I did recently and it was a very scary but incredibly exciting experience. I knew intuitively that it was the right move and intelligently that the risk was a good one, so I went with it. I finally bit the bullet and started to launch my business as a life coach and writer! As a result my WHOLE LIFE began to change. When I say it changed, I mean it started to change that week! Opportunities that I would have turned down in the past I now said YES to. More work in the fields I wanted came my way and I started to get everything I had worked so hard for.

This was by no means easy, as my mind was constantly rattling off asking, "What the . . . ? Why are you doing this? This is insane. Where is the safety and security?" In my heart I knew it was right, though, so I bit the bullet and went for it! What is even better is that I can share this experience with others and assist them in doing the same so they can also get everything they would like for themselves!

Make no mistake, this is not about going on a whim and saying yes to anything and everything. Doing that becomes unconscious in your behaviour and will lead to the same results as you have always experienced. Again, you need to remain responsible for your actions and decisions, so make sure you not only calculate the risk, and feel whether it is the right move, but also if it is the move you need, figure out if you should take it right now.

So you could say there is some contemplation involved, but this is integral to remaining present in the moment, with self-responsible and understanding the consequences of saying yes or no. I did say yes to a lot of opportunities, but also acknowledged that some weren't right for me right now, but will be in six to twelve months. Others were not in line with where I wanted to go, so I did say no.

It is all about remaining open to opportunity that is life! If you remain open to life, things you did not see before suddenly present themselves in a manner that you are now able to finally see them in. Life tests us in many ways, so even when you are open, you do need to keep your smarts about you. You will have opportunities that will be there to fool you; no matter how present or aware you are of what you want and where you want to go and be will affect how frequently you make the right choices. Because there will be many to choose from, you MUST choose wisely. Fail to choose what feels right, and what will bring you to where you want to be will mean you'll need to experience a repeat of this lesson. So as mentioned before, choose wisely!

How does this relate to relationships? It relates in absolutely every way; resisting change will have its consequences, not acknowledging the truth about where your relationship is really at has its consequences as well (another form of resistance). If we remain open in our dealings in life, we will naturally flow into becoming more open in our love life too. By being more open, you will attract someone who truly mirrors what you want in love. A scary step forward, but an exciting one too. By becoming more open, you are choosing not to give power to your fears and therefore trusting yourself in making the right choices for you.

The true meaning of being self-empowered has just been discovered and experienced by YOU!

On your journey forward from here, I send you all my love and support. Your life is about to become more exciting and fulfilling!

THE COMMUNICATION
ERROR/ERA?!

It seems almost comical that in the day and age we are in now, with so much to aid us in communicating to friends, family, locally, nationally, and internationally, that we still seem to have so many misinterpretations and misunderstandings. Surely, it should be as simple as black and white?

Well the straight answer here is NO. Everyone lives in their own reality, so each person's experience of life is completely unique to them and different to any other individual's in the same situation compared to what the next person does is completely different.

So, when we look at basic things like communication, you can start to appreciate why so many people struggle to get their message across and understood in the manner in which it was intended. When it comes to love, there are five languages. Some people use one or two and a few people use all of them. This is how we express our love for someone else. The languages are:

- Words of affirmation
- Quality time
- Gifting
- Offer of service
- Physical touch

Just by reading through these, you will have an idea of what love languages you tend to use most often. Now look at your partner, friends and family; how do they express their love?

So how does this affect our verbal communication/communication as a whole with a potential lover or partner? Have there been times where you have walked away from a date or an encounter with a possible partner feeling more confused than you were before you saw that person? Everyone has at least experienced this feeling once before, both men and women.

It comes from the way we communicate and interpret everyone we encounter. It comes from the way we like to show people we love them and, funnily enough, this actually stems all the way back to our parents and their parents and so on and so forth! We learn our basic abilities in communication from them. This is in no way about blame; it is purely to highlight an understanding of where these things come from and by knowing this you can start to strengthen the aspects that may need work.

Now, let's look at verbal communication. No doubt you have met some people who are very good at communicating verbally from feeling and those who are very good at communicating verbally from logic. When you get two individuals who are great when they communicate verbally from logic, anything to do with feeling and having to express that through verbal communication can be both intimidating and often scary for each person. They are often both wondering if one person is feeling the same as the other and often just wait and bide their time until they know something more and feel comfortable speaking up or both parties actually come together and say something.

The flip side is the expressive verbal communicator. With this type of person, there is no holding back on expressing the way he or she feels, which is great as this makes it very clear to those around that individual just how they feel about them and anything else for that matter. However, this person often can't make sense of logic in regards to "feeling-type interactions," which leaves them often feeling confused as to what actually just happened. Most people who are verbally expressive also get a little carried away in the moment, getting caught up in the dream, drama and fantasy as opposed to reality.

So what can we do to make communication, both the spoken and unspoken word, easier to understand? It starts with us; every unique individual on this planet has a responsibility to him or herself to be more awake to what goes on within as well as outside of their own personal experience.

The more conscious we are of the things we do, the more compassion, understanding, and clarity we will all have in our everyday encounters. Consciousness is the deepest understanding of ourselves and who we are in the world we live in.